**Publishing Credits**

Dona Herweck Rice, *Editor-in-Chief*
Lee Aucoin, *Creative Director*
Kristy Stark, M.A.Ed., *Senior Editor*
Torrey Maloof, *Editor*
Kristine Magnien, M.S.Ed., *Associate
Education Editor*
Neri Garcia, *Senior Designer*
Stephanie Reid, *Photo Researcher*
Rachelle Cracchiolo, M.S.Ed., *Publisher*

**Image Credits**

cover: Thinkstock; pp. 1,4,7,12,15,22,40
iStockphoto; all other images from
Shutterstock.

**Teacher Created Materials**

5301 Oceanus Drive
Huntington Beach, CA 92649-1030
http://www.tcmpub.com
**ISBN 978-1-4333-5267-6**
© 2013 Teacher Created Materials, Inc.

# Table of Contents

# Dear Family,

What a great milestone—you have a kindergartner! You may have heard of the book titled *All I Really Needed to Know I Learned in Kindergarten* by Robert Fulghum. Although there is more to learning than knowing how to share, play fair, and clean up, there is a lot of truth in the notion that this year sets the stage for formal learning. And, the work and learning habits that you help your child establish this year will pay off for the next dozen or more years.

If your child went to day care or preschool, he or she is used to a formal learning setting. If not, there may be a bit of an adjustment period. You'll want to keep in close touch with the teacher so the year goes smoothly. You've been your child's primary teacher for five or so years, and that won't change. This parent guide will give you a variety of parent-tested ideas for having a successful year, beginning with getting organized at home so that your child is ready for the "work" of learning.

## One last thought...

Robert Fulghum includes a lesson about how to live a balanced life. That's good advice for parents, too!

# Getting Off
## to a Great Start

Having a child head off to school may give you some more free time, but those hours fly by. Fortunately, you have a kindergartner who is quite capable of helping each day begin and end smoothly.

## Try these ideas to help your child get organized and stay on task.

### In- and Out-Boxes

Establish a routine for reviewing papers your child brings home. Provide a specific place for teacher notes, school letters, and permission slips. Forms or letters that have to go back to the teacher will go into the out-box.

### Chore Chart

Post a chore chart and establish a completion time to keep your child on task.

### Homework Routine

Your child will have homework that may require your assistance. Remember to let your child take responsibility for his or her homework, but be there as a guide.

## One last thought...

Use a kitchen timer to track the amount of minutes during these work periods. You can get your own work done without managing your child's time.

# *Listen* to Learn

Being able to focus and listen will become increasingly important now that your child attends kindergarten. Good listening skills will make your life easier, too!

## *Practice good listening* with these fun activities.

### Directions

Give a series of directions without stopping, such as clap three times, turn around twice, and touch your toes once. Add activities until your child can do five or six in a series.

### Rhyme Time

Make up a story in rhyme. Provide the first sentence and your child can continue the story by starting a new rhyme.

### Memory Game

For a quick memory game, tell five things about yourself in succession and have your child repeat the five facts. Then, swap turns and keep adding items.

## Rhyming Pairs

Create a set of cards with 15 or more rhyming pairs. Write one word on each card. Deal out four cards each. Player 1 asks, "Do you have a card that rhymes with *bat*?" If so, player 2 gives up the card and player 1 puts down the pair. If not, player 1 draws a card from the deck until he or she has a pair. The game ends when someone has no cards. Count up the pairs for the winner.

**bat**

**cat** **hat**

One last thought...

The memory game makes a great car game, too.

# *Time*
## to Talk!

Your child has learned thousands of words.  Now it's time to keep the conversations going in a more structured fashion.

*Try some of these ideas* to foster thoughtful speaking and more listening.

### Story Book

Have your child look through old magazines and cut out pictures.  Glue each picture on a 5 x 7 inch card: animals, people, houses, and objects. Divide the cards into four stacks, face down.  Have your child make up a story with four cards.  Take a turn and add to the story.

## Picture Cards

Place the picture cards or other pictures in a box or bag. Have your child choose a picture at random and describe it without saying its name. The other players guess what the picture is. After three guesses, add another clue.

## I Spy

Play the game I Spy with your child. Player 1 starts by saying something like, "I spy with my little eye something…little." Player 2 may say something like "Is it yellow?" Player 1 responds appropriately and the game continues until the item is identified.

### One last thought...

These speaking (and listening) games are mostly about having fun. Have your child tell you about the games being learned at school.

# Here's to Sleep
## and Good Health!

Having enough sleep helps your child stay healthy, and helps prepare him or her for a busy day of learning. Young children are at their best early in the morning—and that means they need an early bedtime. Besides having a happy child, you'll have an hour or two to recuperate before your bedtime!

**The chart below shows how much sleep children need**

| Age | Sleep Needed |
| --- | --- |
| 1–3 years | 12–14 hours |
| 3–5 years | 11–13 hours |
| 5–12 years | 10–11 hours |

*These tips* will help your kindergartner get enough sleep:

### Routine

Create a routine with the same bedtime, lighting, and temperature each night.

### Relax

Make it a relaxing time without TV or videos. Instead, read a book in bed before putting your child to sleep.

### Just Say No

Avoid sugary bedtime snacks, especially caffeine.

### Quiet Time

Read aloud a favorite, quiet picture book.

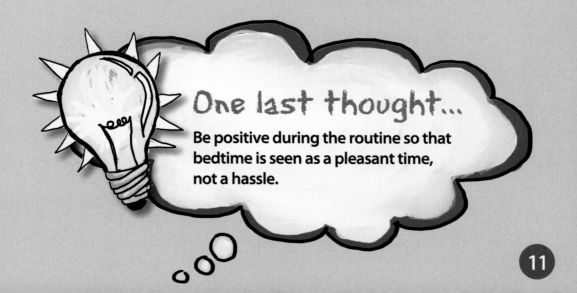

## One last thought...

Be positive during the routine so that bedtime is seen as a pleasant time, not a hassle.

# Top 10
## Things Your Kindergartner
### Needs to Know

1. **Ten basic colors:** red, orange, yellow, green, blue, purple, black, brown, white, and pink

2. **Recognizing and writing the letters** of the alphabet in upper and lowercase

3. **Relationship between letters and the sounds** they make

4. **Sight words 1–100**

5. Writing **consonant-vowel-consonant words** (e.g., bat and fan)

6. **Retelling a story** that has been read aloud

7. Reading and writing **simple sentences**

8. Counting, reading, writing, and comparing **numbers 0–20**

9. **Classifying and counting objects** in categories

10. **Shapes** (e.g., square, triangle, rectangle, circle)

# *Book*
## by Book

Building a home library will continue for many years to come. All the books do not need to be new. Start with your local library to get familiar with books you and your child enjoy.

• • • • • • • • • • • • • • • • • • • • • • • •

## *These ideas* will help you find bargains.

### Book Sales

Watch for library sales, garage sales that specify books, sidewalk sales, and post-season sales. Give your kindergartner a small amount of money so that he or she can make some choices.

### Used Books

Pass along books that your child has outgrown. If your child can't bear to part with them, organize an informal lending library among your neighbors and friends.

### Book Nook

Set up a special place in the house with good lighting, a collection of shelves, bins, or baskets for books, and some comfy pillows. Have your kindergartner help plan the area and keep the books organized.

## One last thought...

As your kindergartner grows up, your home library will grow and change as well. Establishing a joy of reading now will pay off for a lifetime.

# Shared
## Reading

Encourage a new form of sharing—having your child
do more of the reading.

Implement some of *these ideas* to get your
child reading independently.

### Read Aloud

Choose a familiar book and take turns reading aloud each page.  Or
have your child take over the reading of a favorite character's lines.

## Dress Up

Have your child choose a favorite character and dress up accordingly, taking on the character's persona. For example, glue a fur tail and a white chest (of felt or fabric) on a brown t-shirt and you have Foxy Loxy from any version of "Chicken Little."

## Informational Books

Read a set of informational books on a favorite topic, such as insects or dinosaurs.

## Compare and Contrast

Compare traditional tellings of fairy tales to versions with humorous twists, such as Jon Scieszka's *The True Story of the Three Little Pigs by A. Wolf.*

## One last thought...

Your kindergarten teacher or librarian can provide you with recommended reading lists. Make reading aloud a priority.

# Great
# Kindergarten Books

Thousands of children's books are published each year. There are many ways for finding books to help you build a library at home. You probably remember authors from your childhood that you want to share with your child. And, your child probably has a few favorite authors, too!

. . . . . . . . . . . . . . . . . . . . . . . . . . . . . . . . . . . . . . . .

### Here are some books your kindergartner might enjoy.

- *Miss Nelson is Missing* by Harry Allard
- *Stellaluna* by Janell Cannon
- *A Fine, Fine School* by Sharon Creech
- *Click Clack Moo: Cows That Type* by Doreen Cronin
- *Are You My Mother?* by P.D. Eastman
- *Frog and Toad Together* by Arnold Lobel
- *Put Me in the Zoo* by Robert Lopshire
- *If You Give a Mouse a Cookie* by Laura Numeroff
- *Green Eggs and Ham* by Dr. Seuss

Here are some ideas for how to find books.

- Library book sales
- Sales at bookstores
- Garage sales
- Book swap with neighbors

## One last thought...

Kindergarten children love listening to the same books. Check with your librarian for recommended book lists so your child can listen to childhood classics.

# Write

## Starts

Your child will be adding short words to the printing of letters and numbers. Don't expect perfection, those hands are still developing the necessary motor skills. Your kindergartner may love to write little stories, and run all the words together.

Encourage the development of those motor skills with *these ideas*.

### Alphabet Strip

Make an alphabet and number strip or purchase one at a teacher or office supply store. Post it for easy reference.

## Work Center

Have a work center or basket with art supplies, such as finger paints, brushes, and markers. Encourage your child to find creative ways to write his or her name, the dog's name, etc.

## Model Writing

Help strengthen the connection between language and print by modeling writing for your child to see.

## Alphabet Writing

Give your child a piece of waxed paper and a dollop of pudding or a squirt of shaving cream. Encourage your child to use his or her finger to trace the letters of the alphabet.

## Painting Letters

Make paint with a few drops of food coloring and $\frac{1}{4}$ cup of milk. Have your child paint the letter of the day or week on white bread before toasting and eating it.

## One last thought...

Encourage your child to write stories but don't worry about misspellings. Have him or her dictate the story to you while you write it on a sheet of paper.

# Alphabet
## and Letter Formation

Kindergartners are developing their knowledge of letters by recognizing and writing them in upper and lowercase. Practicing the letters of the alphabet will help improve your child's literacy skills.

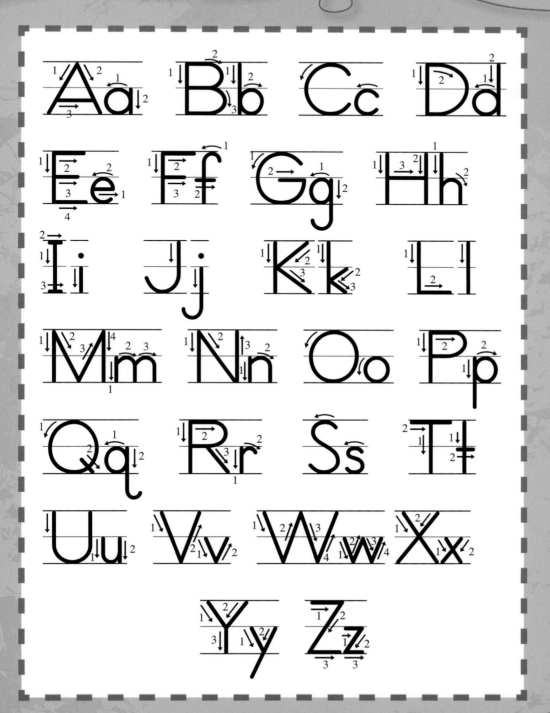

# Math
## Smarts

Does your kindergartner ask for rectangles or triangles when you are cutting a sandwich in half? That simple task involves both shapes and fractions.

• • • • • • • • • • • • • • • • • • • • • • • • • • • • • • • • • • • • •

## Integrate math into your errands and chores with *some of these ideas.*

### Street Signs and Shapes

When you are in a car or on a bus, use street signs to teach the shapes. Keep a tally of how many examples you find of each shape. Once your child knows the basics, have him or her find shapes within shapes.

### Counting to 100

For a variation, choose an object and count until you find 100. Try counting red cars, brown cows, flags, yield signs, churches, etc.

## Counting Backwards

Have your child find numbers on license plates, starting with 20 and find the numbers backwards.

## Market Math

When you are at the grocery store, have your child count, categorize, compare weights, etc. Because we use credit cards so much, we forget that our kids need to learn how to use money. Pay with cash once in a while, involving your child in figuring out the coins and bills.

## One last thought...

Keeping your child involved in tasks such as grocery shopping may slow you down. But, you are building lifelong math skills, expanding vocabulary, and keeping him or her productively busy!

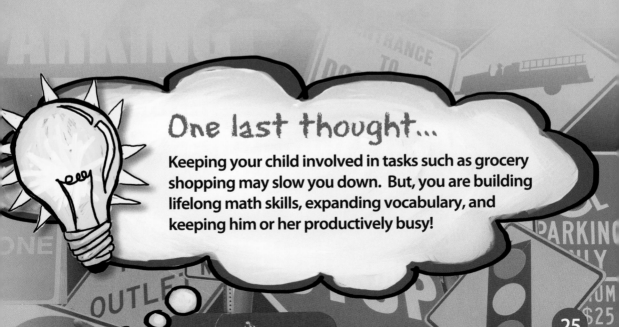

# Math
## at Work

Susan Ohanian once said, "Children need to do what 'real' mathematicians do—explore and invent for the rest of their lives."

Use some of *these ideas* to encourage your budding mathematician.

### Market at Home

When you are cooking dinner, "buy" the ingredients from your pantry by having your kindergartner fetch the cans or boxes you need and sell them to you. Have a jar of coins to make transactions or use play money that is purchased or made.

## Weights

Reinforce the concept of weight by having him or her find the heaviest block.

## Math Books

*The Doorbell Rang* by Pat Hutchins recounts what happens when two kids are ready to share a plate of cookies—and additional people keep joining them. See your library for more ideas, such as *One Hundred Hungry Ants* by Elinor J. Pinczes.

## Sorting and Classifying

Go through your junk drawer or your garage shelves. You have a great collection in the making with which your kindergartner can sort, classify, and create.

## One last thought...

Have your kindergartner help you when cooking or baking. It's a great way to teach fractions and the importance of following directions in the right sequence.

# Number
## Chart 1–20

Kindergartners are expected to master math concepts by using objects that can be counted, classified, and sorted. They are learning that adding means counting forward and subtracting means counting backward. Learning numbers will help improve your child's math skills.

**Practice counting from one to 20 every day!**

| 1 | 2 | 3 | 4 | 5 |
| --- | --- | --- | --- | --- |
| ☆ | ☆ ☆ | ☆ ☆ ☆ | ☆ ☆<br>☆ ☆ | ☆ ☆ ☆<br>☆ ☆ |
| **6** | **7** | **8** | **9** | **10** |
| ☆ ☆ ☆<br>☆ ☆ ☆ | ☆ ☆ ☆<br>☆ ☆ ☆<br>☆ | ☆ ☆ ☆<br>☆ ☆ ☆<br>☆ ☆ | ☆ ☆ ☆<br>☆ ☆ ☆<br>☆ ☆ ☆ | ☆ ☆ ☆<br>☆ ☆ ☆<br>☆ ☆ ☆<br>☆ |

| 11 | 12 | 13 | 14 | 15 |
|---|---|---|---|---|
| ☆ ☆ ☆ | ☆ ☆ ☆ | ☆ ☆ ☆ | ☆ ☆ ☆ | ☆ ☆ ☆ |
| ☆ ☆ ☆ | ☆ ☆ ☆ | ☆ ☆ ☆ | ☆ ☆ ☆ | ☆ ☆ ☆ |
| ☆ ☆ ☆ | ☆ ☆ ☆ | ☆ ☆ ☆ | ☆ ☆ ☆ | ☆ ☆ ☆ |
| ☆ ☆ | ☆ ☆ ☆ | ☆ ☆ ☆ | ☆ ☆ ☆ | ☆ ☆ ☆ |
|  |  | ☆ | ☆ ☆ | ☆ ☆ ☆ |

| 16 | 17 | 18 | 19 | 20 |
|---|---|---|---|---|
| ☆ ☆ ☆ | ☆ ☆ ☆ | ☆ ☆ ☆ | ☆ ☆ ☆ | ☆ ☆ ☆ |
| ☆ ☆ ☆ | ☆ ☆ ☆ | ☆ ☆ ☆ | ☆ ☆ ☆ | ☆ ☆ ☆ |
| ☆ ☆ ☆ | ☆ ☆ ☆ | ☆ ☆ ☆ | ☆ ☆ ☆ | ☆ ☆ ☆ |
| ☆ ☆ ☆ | ☆ ☆ ☆ | ☆ ☆ ☆ | ☆ ☆ ☆ | ☆ ☆ ☆ |
| ☆ ☆ ☆ | ☆ ☆ ☆ | ☆ ☆ ☆ | ☆ ☆ ☆ | ☆ ☆ ☆ |
| ☆ | ☆ ☆ | ☆ ☆ ☆ | ☆ | ☆ ☆ |

# Discoveries
## Unlimited

Your kindergartner has been investigating his or her world since birth. Every new thing was a discovery that had to be tasted, touched, smelled, and watched.

*Try these activities to keep those* discoveries going.

### Listen

Turn a routine walk into a nature sounds walk and listen for animals, birds, the wind, rain, etc.

### Observe

Collect some clean snow in a glass jar and let it melt to see if it still looks clean. Let it evaporate.

## Measure

Plant some seeds and track their growth.

## Explore

Gather a variety of objects, such as light and heavy paper, white and colored paper, clear and colored glass bottles, etc. What happens when they are placed in the sun?

## Touch

Touch things that are smooth, sticky, rough, soft, or hard.

## Journal

Record findings in a notebook with drawings or pictures. Use a camera to document discoveries.

## One last thought...

Keep that wonder about the world alive by staying alert to opportunities to stop and observe, touch, and discuss.

# The Social
## Community

Your child's world is steadily expanding from your friends and family to the community at large. Kindergarten is the ideal time to deepen your child's understanding of community workers and their importance.

*Encourage a deeper understanding of* people and their roles with these activities.

### Community Workers

Have a dress-up box or chest with props, such as a fireman's hat, police officer's badge, tote bag full of junk mail, apron, chef's hat, etc. Watch the newspapers for announcements of an open house at the firehouse, a factory, or the post office.

## Construction Building

Watching the construction of a building is a great way to introduce your child to a variety of vehicles and associated workers: carpenters, plumbers, electricians, and truck drivers.

## Culture and Tradition

Your child will be learning about different cultures at school, making this the perfect time to learn about different foods. Ask a relative or neighbor to cook a traditional meal. Plan to try a new ethnic food once a month or visit an ethnic restaurant.

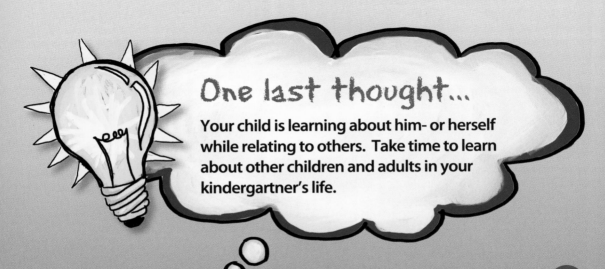

One last thought...

Your child is learning about him- or herself while relating to others. Take time to learn about other children and adults in your kindergartner's life.

# After-School
## Fun

Your kindergartner, if in a half-day program, will undoubtedly have some energy left after class. Discuss with him or her which kind of classes are appealing, such as music, art, sports, or dance.

*Start with one,* and if that goes well, *add another one* later in the year.

### Art

Check with children's museums and libraries for classes that explore art. Some classes combine art with science or nature study.

### Sports

Your recreation center, sports centers, YWCA, or YMCA may offer a variety of sports lessons. Choose a sport that is of interest and emphasizes learning the skills while having fun.

## Drama

Look for opportunities at community drama centers if your child has an interest in acting or storytelling.

## One last thought...

Do you have a special talent or interest? Consider gathering children and having an informal weekly gathering to explore your hobby.

# Learning
## on the Go

You probably spend a fair amount of time in the car. Take advantage of time with your child and learn something new together.

• • • • • • • • • • • • • • • • • • • • • • • • • • • • • • • • • • •

## Keep your child busy—and learning—with *some of these activities.*

### Scavenger Hunt

Give your child a list of things that can be seen for an on-the-go scavenger hunt. Put the list on a clipboard and tie on a pencil for checking off the items.

### Who Am I?

Play the "Who Am I?" game. Think of a friend, relative, favorite toy, cartoon character, etc. Give a hint such as, "It is green and fuzzy." Let everyone guess once. Give another hint if no one guesses correctly. Then, pass the turn.

## Travel Games

Create a backpack that contains favorite activities that are only for travel: magnetic games, tic-tac-toe, squishy balls to squeeze, favorite CDs, etc.

## Treasure Bottle

Prepare a treasure bottle. Take a clean jar and fill it about $\frac{3}{4}$ full with uncooked rice and 25 small objects: buttons, nails, dice, coins, and beads. Keep a list of the items. Tighten the lid securely (or seal it with some glue). Give it to your child to turn and shake to find all the items. Keep track—can he or she find them all?

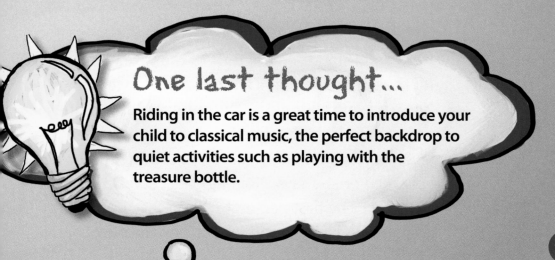

## One last thought...

Riding in the car is a great time to introduce your child to classical music, the perfect backdrop to quiet activities such as playing with the treasure bottle.

# Play
## Each Day!

Even though your child is in school, play continues to be an important part of his or her life. And it should be fun for you too. After all, that's one of the best things about having a child—you get to play, too!

● ● ● ● ● ● ● ● ● ● ● ● ● ● ● ● ● ● ● ● ● ● ● ● ● ● ● ● ● ● ● ● ●

*Try some of these ideas* for group games with family members and neighbors.

### Cyclops Tag

Everyone plays with one hand covering an eye.

### Skunk Tag

Players are "safe" by standing in one of four hula hoops designated as a safety zone. Only one person is allowed in the hoop at a time and for no longer than 20 seconds.

### Red Light, Green Light

One child stands on one side of the yard, while the rest of the family members and neighbors face him or her from the opposite side. The child standing alone is the "traffic light." When he or she says, "Green light," everyone is allowed to take steps toward him or her, and when he or she says, "Red light," everyone must stop moving. The first person to reach the "traffic light" win and gets to be the "traffic light" for the next round.

# One last thought...

**Take time to enjoy outings with your family,
even if it is a quick trip to the local park.**

Thank you for taking time to read this book. We hope that you found some new ideas or were reminded that what you are doing as a parent is very important to your child's learning. Keep in touch with your child's teacher and other adults in his or her life. Everyone wants to ensure that your child has a great year in kindergarten.

Before you know it, the year will be finished and you'll be looking at a first grader! Enjoy the journey—being a parent is the most important job in the world.

*Thank you!*